FRED BASSET

2022

FRED BASSET YEARBOOK 2022

Drawings by Michael Martin

An Hachette UK Company
www.hachette.co.uk

Summersdale Publishers Ltd
Part of Octopus Publishing Group Limited
Carmelite House
50 Victoria Embankment
LONDON
EC4Y 0DZ
UK

www.summersdale.com

Printed and bound in the Czech Republic

ISBN: 978-1-80007-003-5

FRED!
That wasn't a very good start!
My New Year's Resolution was to stop barking just for the sake of it!

I HAVE CONVERTED MY OLD SHED — COME AND HAVE A LOOK!
NOW I CAN DO ALL MY PUSH-UPS, SIT-UPS AND WEIGHTLIFTING IN HERE!
What a great idea — He should do the same!
Post-festivities and all that...?!

1
4
2
MRM
We could be in for a long evening!
SEVEN!
501 501

FRED!
Ooops!
I was miles away!
MRM

FRED
For some it may be the beginning of an exciting New Year –
But around here it is business as usual !
I am nipping into my local for a drink !
At the moment, Jock just happens to be local !
JOCK

Strong and stable—
That's me!

VETERINARY CLINIC
I pity the vet with this lot!
ME-OW
SQUAWK
SQUEAK

Come on — You can do it!
Their first tentative steps!
OH, ANN — THEY'RE ADORABLE!

OH—SO YOU WANT A WALK, DO YOU?!
That's not quite the response I was hoping for!
But at least it's not a no!

What a week poor old Jock has had— His bone was stolen, his new bouncy ball burst and then he came a disappointing fourth place in the local dog show—
He could do with some counselling!
Do you want to play ball, Jock?
Obviously not—
He didn't bat an eyelid!
M&M
M&M

I'M SO LATE!
'BYE, DEAR!
He certainly went out with a bang!

BEEP BEEP — OUT OF THE WAY!
Little hoodlum!
BEEP BEEP BRUM BRUM

WOOF
YIP
Stunned into silence!

OH MY GOODNESS—IT'S POURING DOWN!
Tell me about it!

Well behaved — Well mannered — Well groomed —
I am the perfect role model!
MBM

It's all very well being a role model —
But keeping it up is rather tiresome!
MBM

OH, A BASSET—I'VE HEARD THAT THEY'RE RATHER STUBBORN AND NOTORIOUSLY DIFFICULT TO TRAIN?
NO OFFENCE OF COURSE!
MBM
NONE TAKEN!
Speak for yourself!!

DINNER, FRED!
MBM
STEAK AND KIDNEY PIE, CHIPS AND PEAS!
I don't take any notice—
THERE WE ARE, SIR—ENJOY—AND TO FOLLOW, BLACK FOREST GÂTEAU WITH CREAM!
I just humour him!
FRED

Share and share alike ?
Too late !
I'm popping round to the Barrington-Smyths. Apparently they have two new puppies !
I shall report back shortly !

FRED'S KEEN THIS MORNING!
Yes, I am!
IT SEEMS AS IF HE IS TAKING US FOR A WALK!
Yes, I am!
HE SEEMS TO KNOW WHERE HE'S GOING!
Yes, I do!
The Barrington-Smyths have two new puppies!
Aren't they just adorable?!
AREN'T THEY JUST ADORABLE?!
Just look at their cute little faces!
JUST LOOK AT THEIR CUTE LITTLE FACES!
We are a soppy lot, aren't we?!
AHHH!
YIP
YIP
YIP
YIP
YIP

The Barrington-Smyths' new puppies are soooo sweet!
YIP YIP YIP YIP YIP YIP
When is our first playdate?!
YIP YIP
BE GENTLE, FRED!
How can I be anything but?!
YIP YIP YIP YIP YIP YIP

WHAT'S UP WITH FRED?
Barrington-Smyths! Barrington-Smyths!
I THINK HE WANTS HIS WALK!
Barrington-Smyths! Barrington-Smyths!
I THINK HE WANTS TO SEE THOSE PUPPIES AGAIN!
He's got it! He's got it!

OH, HE WAS NO PROBLEM, ANN!
Yorky is off home!
YIP YIP YIP YIP
HE IS MORE THAN WELCOME TO COME AND STAY ANY TIME – 'BYE, ANN, 'BYE, YORKY!
Steady on, dear –
It was okay having him to stay but I'm not so sure about the *any time* bit!!

Are you ready to take on the Grosvenor Avenue Gang, lads?
The Formidable Foursome!

YES, OF COURSE WE CAN LOOK AFTER YORKY FOR THE WEEK— NO, IT'S NOT A PROBLEM AT ALL!
A week??
FRED WILL LOVE IT—WON'T YOU FRED!
Um... I know he's my friend and all that...
OK, ANN—WE'LL SEE YOU BOTH TOMORROW. 'BYE!
...but a week may be pushing it!

At the mere mention of a walk —
Yorky launches into hyper-mode!
YIP YIP YIP YIP YIP YIP YIP YIP YIP YIP YIP YIP
YIP YIPPY YIP YIP YIP YIP YIP YIP
By nature I am not a cat lover...
... but sometimes I surprise myself!
PURRRRRRR
PURRRRRRR

Ok, Yorky—Enough is enough!
You are pushing your luck too far!
FRED
FR
I hereby terminate your staycation!
FRED
COME ON, FRED—OVER YOU HOP!
Over I hop?
What a preposterous suggestion!

There it is, Yorky—
A feast for your eyes!
It's little Amanda's birthday tomorrow—
The production line is in full swing!

Amanda's birthday—
Bedlam!
I'm off!

Yorky is of a nervous disposition—
Boo!
YIP
Naughty old me!

It is an unenviable position being a whistleblower –
OH, COME OFF IT, REF. !
BOO !

YIP YIP
YIP
YIPPY YIP
YIP
YIP YIP
YIP
YIP
YIP
YIP
Spring has sprung and so have we !
YAP YAP
YAPPY YAP
YAP
YAP
YAP
YAP
YAP

They make it look so easy!
YIP YIP
YAP YAP

Oh!
Oh!
Now *that* is music to my ears!

DINNER'S READY!
STEAK AND KIDNEY PIE!
MMM... SMELLS LOVELY, DEAR!
My hopes are dashed!

A nifty piece of footwork from Yorky!

READY, STEADY— GO!
Our boat race!
Are you feeling invincible lads?
Good—Hold on to that feeling!

I wonder if he has forgiven me yet for digging up his vegetable patch this morning?
COME HERE, YOU!
As I thought—
He's just a big softie!
Yorky—I wouldn't if I were you!
ZZZ
Never trouble trouble...
M&M

WHAT'S THE MATTER, FRED? GO AND FETCH YOUR BALL!
If he thinks I am going to enter uncharted territory...
... he has got another think coming!
This is what you call an international line-up!

FRED!
We have had a bone-related incident—
He tripped on it, and—

Not today, thank you—
By appointment only!

GUESS WHAT, DEAR—FRED JUMPED THE STREAM IN ONE LEAP!
Well ?
Stunned disbelief!
What did I come out here for ?
I'm losing the plot!

UNIDENTIFIED ITEM
Unidentified ?!
But everyone knows me – I'm Fred – Fred Basset!
GET DOWN, FRED!

OH LOOK, IT'S FRED THE BASSET!
On a dull day like this my personality shines through!
WHAT A HAPPY CHAPPY!
HE'S A CHEERFUL CHAP, ISN'T HE?!
LOOK, HE'S WAGGING HIS TAIL!

Here's one …
… and another —
THANKS, FRED !
THANKS, FRED !
I have a nose for this !
Ok lads — The long way home …
… or the short way home with the risk of bumping into those terriers at number twenty nine ?
We'll play safe !

This is not my normal type of outing—
I stole some sausages from the butchers and he's dragging me down there to apologise!
I guess it's more of a guilt trip!

DINNER, FRED!
Great—I'm ravenous!
FRED
FRED
Somewhat scant, I fear!
FRED

For goodness' sake, Yorky!
If our biscuit mission is to succeed...
...we must adopt the softly softly approach!
MGM
Taffy and Yorky?
They're more like Dilly and Dally!
MGM

Mrs. Johnson's cat !!
N.I.M.B.I. !!
Not In My Best Interest !
MBM

Ooops !
Inappropriate footwear, a slippery stone...
... and a dash of foolhardiness thrown in !
MBM

Loopy and I have a lot in common !

As I thought — Their latest diet ...
... was just a passing fad !
COFFEE ÉCLAIR OR CREAM DOUGHNUT ?
UMMM...?

There are two sides to every story!
M&M

THIS NEW DOG FOOD OF FRED'S IS SUPPOSED TO BE VERY NUTRITIOUS!
Nutritious?
FRED
And delicious!!
FRED
M&M

I wonder what he's preparing for —
The Tour d' Angleterre ?!
Rose & Crown
Happy hour !

Leftovers ?
FRED
Inedible !
FRED

Here comes the Grosvenor Avenue Gang, lads —
Action stations !

YES, OF COURSE YOU CAN, JENNY— FRED WON'T MIND!
I feel a bit put upon!
GIDDY UP, FRED!

It's nearly my dinner time!
E.T.A. — Six o'clock!
I should just make it!

MAY WE HAVE A BOWL OF WATER FOR OUR DOG, PLEASE?
YES, NO PROBLEM!
Oh good!
I don't like being a problem!

The trouble with rabbits is—
They all have *hidey-holes*!

COME ON, FRED — JUMP !
Jump ?
Get real, mate !

YAP YIP YAP YIP
BARK BARK
If you can't say anything nice — Don't say anything at all !

A BIRTHDAY TREAT, DEAR — BREAKFAST IN BED!
With today's Fred Basset strip to follow!

YIP YAP
YAP YIP YAP YIP
YIP YAP YIP YAP
YAP YAP
YIP YIP YIP
Oh to be young!

... HE MAKES A PASS ...
... HE HEADS IT IN —
GOAL !
YES !
OUCH !!
Caution: always be sure that the air above is empty before punching it !
DO BE CAREFUL, DEAR !

FRED — DO YOU HAVE TO BARK LIKE THAT FIRST THING IN THE MORNING ?
WOOF
WOOF
WOOF
Sorry, mate — Standard practice !
WOOF
WOOF
WOOF

Delicious—
FRED
But hardly the main event!
FRED
... firms and regenerates—for a smoother and younger-looking appearance!
I wonder?!

Hi, Yorky!
Someone is a bit tetchy this morning!
M&M

Do excuse us—Jock and I are having a…
… tête-à-tête!
M&M

What a show-stopper !

You know things are bad ...
... when you encounter gridlock getting out of your own driveway !

Me? Stolen your bone??
I exercise the right to silence!
M&M
I'm right behind you, lads —
Power on, Fred!
M&M

WHAT NONSENSE — I HAVE NEVER HEARD SUCH RUBBISH !
WHAT THEY SHOULD BE DOING IS . . .
An armchair expert !

Ah, Jock, Yorky — there you are !
I was aware of a noticeable absence !

WOOF!
WOOF — A SOUND USUALLY ASSOCIATED WITH A DOG —
I wish they would turn that thing off before they go out!

Poor little Yorky — He's completely overshadowed —

FRED!
FR—ED!
Yes, one moment!
You called?!
M&M

It's nearly six o'clock and there's no sign of my dinner yet!
M&M
I hope she hasn't forgotten!
HERE YOU ARE, FRED!
She has certainly cut it a bit fine!
FRED

Mmm... sausages!
?!
You will be pleased to know that I thought better of it!
M&M
Cat in the garden!
WOOF WOOF WOOF
Rapid about-turn required!
MEE-OW
MEE-OW
MEE-OW
M&M

Jock has had a mishap with his new trick!
He won't be trying that again any time soon!
MBM

You want me to jump?!
Jock is the eternal optimist!
MBM

WOOF WOOF
WOOF
Yorky!
WOOF
Every little helps!
WOOF
WOOF
YIP
YIP YIP
M&M

YAWN
YAWN
Infectious!
YAWN
M&M

The butcher's van has broken down in Wickham Avenue?
Jump to it, lads —
An opportunity like this comes once in a lifetime!
M&M

Jock, have you seen my bone?
You're not at liberty to say?
Yorky, have you seen it?
Your right to silence?
I smell a conspiracy!
M&M

The boys' hockey team has finally met its match —
The girls' hockey team !!
YiP YiP
YaP YaP
My dream came true !
YaP
YaP
YiP
YiP

Here is Big Bruce, lads, returning from his mission to the butcher's!
I wonder how he got on?
His expression says it all!

Wrong place, wrong time!
Right place, right time!
HERE YOU ARE, FRED!
FRED

It may not be much, but I am content with what I've got –
My worldly possessions!
FRED
Yes, Jock—I appreciate that it's one of your favourite bones...
... and yes, normally I would be only too happy to help...
... but, unfortunately, I think you can wave goodbye to it!

WHERE'S FRED?
En plein-air!
... YOU'RE ON THE TRAIN? OK, SEE YOU SHORTLY!
My cue!

We came across the Grosvenor Avenue Gang on our little jaunt through Tinkers Wood –
The result ?
A verdict of misadventure !

F.B. and the T.T.s out for a stroll with M. and M. –
Fred Basset, Tucker Twins, Master and Mistress !

FR–ED!
Yes–In a minute!
FRED—HERE!!
Uh oh–I had better go!
That's his authoritative voice!
What a lovely sight– A happy family–
Scooting along!

DO YOU FANCY A GAME OF BASEBALL, LADS?
You bet—We were born for it!
I'll be first baseman. Jock, you can be second baseman. Taffy, you can be third baseman...
... and Yorky, you can be shortstop!
WELL?
Brill!
FRED
FRED

COME ON THEN, FRED, BRING IT ON !
GRRRRRR
GRRRRRRR
Don't worry, folks — It's only a play-fight!
HA HA HA HA
MGM

I've just seen a slithering snake !
Need I say more ?!
MGM

NOT FAR NOW TO THE TOP!
COME ON, FRED!
Ever onward and upward!
MSM

WOOF WOOF
That's Bert!
It takes one to know one!
MSM

ON YOUR MARKS
I'm not keen on bangs...
GET SET
...so it's a jumping-the-gun moment!

READY, FRED?
Yep!
STEADY, FRED?
Yep!
GO, FRED!
I've gone!

HERE HE IS!
HAPPY BIRTHDAY, FRED!
HE'S SUCH A LOVELY CHAP!
Still sparkling after all these years!
GOOD OLD FRED!

HEY, FRED — COME BACK WITH OUR BALL!
Who's a naughty ballboy, then?!

YIP
Whoops!
That looks like a good idea! I think I'll join them—
FRED

He's having to work hard—
He has met his match!

Dodgy bulb needs changing in the kitchen!

I have called for a conference—
A *summit* conference!
Bert and I do like a laugh!

Fred the sausage-stealer strikes again!
Not my best claim to fame!
... AND NOW CONTESTANT NUMBER THREE —
DOG SHOW
All eyes on me, please!

WHIMPER
WHIMPER
WOOF
Sorry, but...

IT WAS WORTH THE CLIMB, DEAR — WHAT A BREATHTAKING VIEW!
Breathtaking indeed!

Here it comes...
Here it comes—
Good morning sunshine!
Peek-a-boo!
I can see yoooou!

This makes a pleasant change from chasing rabbits!
Mmm... Sausages for the taking!
Stand back, lads— Equal opportunites and all that—
Fifi—Over to you!

... I SPY WITH MY LITTLE EYE ...
Oh no!
... SOMETHING BEGINNING WITH ...
I do wish the breakdown people would hurry up!
Come on, Fred— Up and over!
A little overambitious but here goes!
YAP
YIP

A dab of this and a dab of that–
COME ON, FRED!
Now we're ready to face the world!
MGM
What a lovely view!
Poor old Yorky. He could do with an upgrade–
MGM
Come on, lad!

You're going to risk life and limb and stroll in there to get your bone back ?
I've got to see this !
Well I never–I am dumbfounded !
ZZZZ
M&M
A lovely day out watching the scenery go by. With the gentle swaying and the clickety-clack...
... I'm feeling rather zzzzzzz.....
M&M

LOOK, DEAR—FRED HAS BEEN INVITED TO JOCK'S BIRTHDAY PARTY— WHAT FUN!
YORKY AND THE REST OF THE GANG WILL BE THERE TOO!
Acceptance on its way!

COME ON, FRED—IT'S NOT FAR TO THE TOP!
Not for me, thanks—
I prefer to stay at base camp!

Jock's birthday bash is certainly catering for everyone!
There they all are—
Hello, everyone!
My circle of friends!

Unlike Jock and Yorky—
I am a natural!

OH LOOK, DEAR, A WEDDING INVITATION— FRED, JOCK AND YORKY ARE INVITED TOO!
And Fifi and Jemma?!

A U.F.O. ?
A close encounter ?
My mistake—Just a passing cumulus !

OH DEAR—FRED LOOKS REALLY HOT AND BOTHERED !
I have just been chased all the way down Church Street by Mrs. Burton's terrier... and... on a scorching day like today...
... yes... it's safe to say that I **am** really hot and bothered !!

IT LOOKS AS IF FRED IS COMING TO JOIN US!
You bet I am—
I'm feeling groovy!
WOOF WOOF
Note to self: pick on someone your own size!!
YIP YIP YIP YIP YIP YIP

Look out, lads—
Too late !
Wake up, man !!
It's the only thing he has had to do all afternoon !
CATCH !

I AM REALLY LOOKING FORWARD TO OUR LITTLE BREAK!
ME TOO!
A painting holiday!
Mind you– He has only just finished the hallway–
You would think the last thing he would want to do is *more* painting!
DON'T FORGET YOUR EASEL, DEAR!
He seems to have settled in nicely!
ART COURSE STARTS HERE TODAY
WE'RE OFF FOR A WALK, WOULD YOU LIKE TO JOIN US?
We'll leave him to it!

We're off for a bit of painting en plein-air today—
THIS LOOKS LIKE A LOVELY SPOT!
That's if they're still up for it?!
They are attempting landscape watercolour today—
Unfortunately, more water than colour!

THAT IS LOOKING LOVELY, DEAR!
They have created quite an audience!
MOOO

It's raining, so he has been reduced to painting a still life indoors—
Me!

JUST LOOK AT THIS RUSH HOUR TRAFFIC!
Rush hour?
It doesn't seem as if anyone is rushing anywhere!
AND WHAT DO YOU THINK YOU'RE DOING, FRED?
I am doing a bit of basking!

Afternoon tea on the terrace?
How very civilised!
He has succumbed to temptation —
BUT YOU'VE ONLY JUST FINISHED LUNCH, DEAR!
Hot Dogs

They have been clearing out the attic...
HOW ABOUT THIS, DEAR?
YEP!
... and off to the boot-fair we go!
It's sad to see my old puppy basket go...
IT'S PERFECT, DEAR!
OH YES — BUBBLES WILL LOVE IT!
YIP
...but I have a feeling that it's going to a good home!

Yorky!
Oops — Too late!

Back to school for the Tucker Twins —
That has taken the spring out of their step!

OH, FRED —
HOW COULD YOU ?!
I was spurred on !
MSM

Introvert !
Extrovert !
MSM

Jock — Steady on ...
Yorky — Calm down ...
Let's try to find some central ground!

DO YOU FANCY A WALK ALONG THE CANAL, DEAR?
YES—THAT WOULD BE NICE!
It's a yes from her and a yes from me!

HAVE YOU TRIED A SLICE OF THE CAKE I MADE, DEAR?
YES – I HAD A SMALL SLICE, THANK YOU!
A small slice?!
A little economical with the truth!

I'm in need of a breather!
Bring on the substitute!

WE'RE JUST POPPING OUT FOR A DRINK AT THE BARRINGTON-SMYTH'S, FRED!
WHIMPER
SORRY, BOY—WE CAN'T TAKE YOU WITH US!
I don't want to go with them—
WHIMPER
I want my dinner before they go!
WHIMPER

There is not much hope of getting our ball back, lads—
It has gone with the flow!

OH FRED!
No need to thank me—
Bluebottle successfully removed!
DINNER, FRED!
Hey—Hang on a minute!
I don't recall inviting you lot!

Here come Titan and the vicar —
The great and the good!
FOR HEAVEN'S SAKE, TITAN — SLOW DOWN!

Nothing in life is certain . . .
DINNER, FRED!
. . . so there is always a sense of relief when my dinner arrives!
FRED

DID YOU ENJOY THAT, FRED?
FRED
A triumph!
FRED
Ooo-er!
Jock—A leadership vacancy has become available!
Over to you!

OUR TURN, FRED!
Ooo-er!
AGILITY CLASS
Phew!
BASSET AGILITY CLASS
Mixed ability?
Dog Show
Mixed ability class
That sums us lot up perfectly!

The outright winner is Fred the Basset!
The crowd goes wild for this champion of champions!
They rise to their feet as he steps forward to claim the prestigious prize!
I can dream can't I?!

Just look at Jock—
Conceited or what?!
1ST

Oh look —
A modern-day Noah!
COME ALONG, YOU TWO!

READY, LADS?
I'm not taking any chances!

DO YOU WANT TO GO OUT, FRED?
Yep!
I have the whole world to greet!!
WOOF
WOOF
WOOF
WOOF
WOOF
Please excuse my lopsidedness, folks —
A-hem!

ARE YOU READY YET?
NEARLY!
YOU SAID THAT TWENTY MINUTES AGO!
I'LL BE RIGHT DOWN!
COME ON—WE'RE GOING TO BE LATE!
COMING...
I think I know what you were thinking ?!
M&M

BEEP
Yorky has gone hi-tech!
M&M

An old coat, a blanket and a few bits and bobs—
She has hidden talents!
On a chilly morning like this—
I am the envy of the neighbourhood!

I have a playdate !
Here comes Jock trying to impress us with his latest trick—
A passing fad !

WALK, FRED!
?
I need some motivation!
We've got to try and lose him, lads—
Let's go off-road!

HOW ABOUT THE LOSER BUYS THE NEXT ROUND ?
This could cost him dear !
MSM

I'M READY, FRED !
Here I come — Catch me !
She caught me !
MSM

...AND WHAT HAS FRED BEEN UP TO TODAY, THEN?
NOT MUCH!
fredbeen@home.comfy.uk.thanks
M&M
Uh oh!
M&M
How's that for a sidestep?!

Black ice ?!

... IT HAS BEEN LOVELY TALKING TO YOU, ARABELLA, BUT WE MUST GO—DO KEEP IN TOUCH!
Public persona!
IT HAS BEEN LOVELY TALKING TO YOU TOO, DARLINGS—'BYE FOR NOW!
WHAT A DREADFUL WOMAN!
ISN'T SHE JUST—POKING HER NOSE INTO OTHER PEOPLE'S BUSINESS!
Private persona!

MRS. JOHNSON'S CAT IS IN OUR GARDEN, FRED — DO YOU WANT TO GO AND CHASE IT AWAY ?
Not really !
It's not high on my agenda today !
He's all fired up !
PASS THE SAUSAGES, DEAR !

HOW DO YOU RATE THE NEW DOGGYDINS, THEN, FRED ?
FRED
FRED

A glimpse into the future ?

Come on, Yorky –
We can do it!
It's a joint effort!

NOT YET, FRED!
But...
LET THEM SETTLE DOWN FIRST!
But...
... it's the puppies' first trip to the park and I don't want to miss out!
YIP YIP
YIP YIP

Hide and seek ?
Best of luck, mate !
MSM

Yes, Jock, it is very picturesque ...
... but that doesn't mean that I want to go out in it !
MSM

FRED—WHAT DO YOU THINK YOU'RE DOING ?!
Helping ?
Pixie, Trixie, I wouldn't if I were you !
This is not going to end well !
YIP
YIP
YIP
YIP
YIP
YIP
YIP
YIP
YIP

Lucky old me—After a fun-filled day with the Tucker Twins—
I get a lift home!
M&M
ANY ROOM FOR ME ON THE SOFA?!
M&M
Nope!
CHOC DROPS

Oops !
Don't stand on ceremony, pups —
Tuck in !
YIP
YIP